CONTENTS

THAT'S IMPOSSIBLE!

If you want to amaze your friends and family, show them a few fantastic magic tricks! Professional magicians spend years learning fiendishly tricky moves, but there are all kinds of simple magic skills that you can learn – with a little practice.

◄ *You'd need fancy equipment to be able to stage spectacular tricks like this!*

▼ *Some magicians use **gimmicks** such as rings that look solid, but link together.*

Types of magic

There are many types of magic. Some stage magicians use big, lavish props to create incredible **illusions**, such as **levitating** or making entire buildings disappear. Other magicians prefer close-up magic, such as making coins appear or disappear in front of you. Some magicians pretend to read minds instead.

MAGIC
SKILLS

STEPHANIE TURNBULL

W
FRANKLIN WATTS
LONDON • SYDNEY

An Appleseed Editions book

Paperback edition 2014

First published in 2012 by Franklin Watts
338 Euston Road, London NW1 3BH

Franklin Watts Australia
Hachette Children's Books
Level 17/207 Kent St, Sydney, NSW 2000

© 2012 Appleseed Editions

Created by Appleseed Editions Ltd,
Well House, Friars Hill, Guestling,
East Sussex TN35 4ET

Designed and illustrated by Guy Callaby
Edited by Mary-Jane Wilkins
Photo research by Su Alexander

ISBN 978 1 4451 3178 8

Dewey Classification: 793.8

All words in **bold** can be found in the Glossary on page 30.

Website information is correct at the time of going to press. However, the publishers
cannot accept liability for any information or links found on third-party websites.

A CIP catalogue for this book is available from the British Library.

Picture credits
l = left, r = right, t = top, b = bottom, c = centre
Page 2 l Dibrova/Shutterstock, r PzAxe/Shutterstock; 3 Fotosutra.com/Shutterstock;
4l Natalia Bratslavsky/Shutterstock, r Jaimie Duplass/Shutterstock; 5 Thor Jorgen
Udvang/Shutterstock; 6,8,9 & 10 Thinkstock; 11 Ben Bryant/Shutterstock;
14 Hemera Technologies/Thinkstock; 15 Thinkstock; 16 Steve Cukrov/Shutterstock;
18 Thinkstock; 20 Koratmember/Shutterstock; 22 Thinkstock; 24 Comstock/
Thinkstock; 26 Thinkstock; 27l Akva/Shutterstock, r Stephani Lupoli/Shutterstock;
28 Thinkstock & Shutterstock; 29l Hung Chung Chih/Shutterstock, r Jack Q/
Shutterstock; 30t Macgyverhh/Shutterstock, b Kurhan/Shutterstock; 31t Thinkstock,
b Shutterstock

Front cover: playing cards Korionov, wand Kelly Richardson,
coins Roman Sigaev, all images Shutterstock

Printed in China

Franklin Watts is a division of Hachette Children's Books,
an Hachette UK company.
www.hachette.co.uk

Three golden rules

If you want to be a great magician, remember these three golden rules.

1. Never perform a trick until you're ready. If you're not sure what to do, or don't feel confident, the trick may not work properly.

2. Never do a trick twice. People will be looking harder the second time, and may figure out your method.

3. Never reveal how a trick is done. It spoils all the mystery! Also, because many tricks are really very simple, people may be disappointed once they hear the secret.

▲ *A magician performs eye-catching Japanese magic tricks at a festival. Outdoor magic like this is called street magic.*

SUPER ★ FACTS

★ One famous magician was the French conjuror Jean Eugène Robert-Houdin (1805-71). He created his own props and performed stunning shows with all kinds of spectacular illusions.

★ Magicians who join magic societies must promise never to reveal secrets of magic to non-magicians.

★ Some modern magicians, such as Penn and Teller, tease the audience by pretending to show how tricks are done – before adding new twists that leave people even more baffled!

MAGIC BASICS

There are two kinds of tricks: self-working tricks, which work every time, as long as you do things in a certain way, and sleight of hand tricks (sleights for short), which involve learning sneaky moves. You need the same basic skills for both.

◀ Complex prop tricks rely on misdirecting the audience's attention.

Look at this (not at that)

One vital magic skill is misdirection – in other words, deliberately drawing the audience's attention away from things you don't want them to notice or think too much about. This way you can make them think something impossible has happened. You can misdirect using what you say (called **patter**) and body language.

Try this misdirection. In a café with a friend, take a salt packet and toss it casually in front of you, close to the edge of the table.

Start to scoop up the packet, but slide it towards you and let it fall in your lap. Misdirect your friend's attention by talking and looking at your fist, as if you are holding the salt.

Blow on your fist and open it to reveal that the salt has gone.

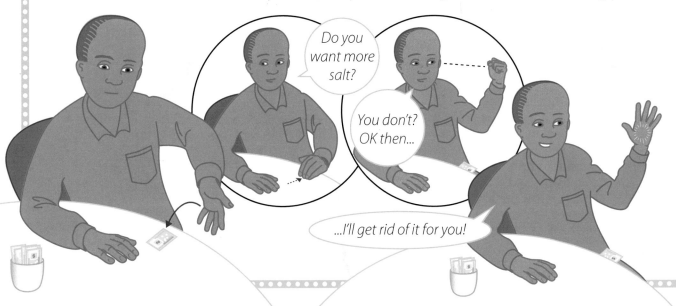

Do you want more salt?

You don't? OK then...

...I'll get rid of it for you!

Go for it!

You need confidence to do magic. You may worry that a trick is so simple that people will spot the secret straight away – but remember, they don't know as much as you! If you practise beforehand, misdirect attention and act confidently, your tricks will be really effective.

Make 'em laugh

Don't forget that humour helps to entertain people. For example, you could alter the vanishing salt trick and pretend to push the packet into your ear.

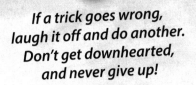

If a trick goes wrong, laugh it off and do another. Don't get downhearted, and never give up!

While you're misdirecting attention to your ear, sneakily pick up the salt packet and hide it in your other hand. Now cough into the hand and open it to reveal the salt!

Short and sweet

As a beginner, it's a good idea to perform just one or two tricks at once. Do them casually, for example while at a bus stop or waiting for a class to start. This way, people will be more surprised and impressed than if you make a big fuss of wanting to show a trick.

PERFECT PROPS

Getting started with magic doesn't mean spending a fortune at a joke shop on fancy gimmicks. The best equipment is everyday stuff you can find at home. Here are some ideas to start with.

Escaping Rubber Band

All you need for this easy trick are a couple of rubber bands.

1. Hold up your hand, palm facing you, and put a rubber band over your index and middle fingers. Tell a friend it's a magical jumping band.

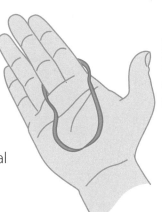

2. As you talk, stretch the band towards you with your other hand, and curl all four fingers into the loop.

Your friend doesn't see this.

3. Hold up your fist. Say a magic word or blow on it, then quickly open your hand. The band will jump on to the other two fingers!

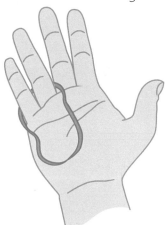

4. Put the band back on the first two fingers and say that this time you'll trap it in place. Wind another rubber band around your fingertips.

5. Now do step 2 and 3 in exactly the same way. The band still jumps!

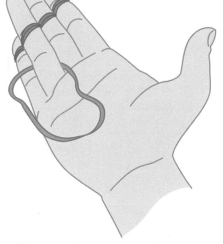

Paper Clip Flip

Here's another fun self-working trick.

1. Put two paper clips and a bank note on the table. Tell a friend you'll give them the note if they can link the paper clips – but without touching the clips together.

2. When they say it's impossible, take the bank note and fold it into an 's' shape like this.

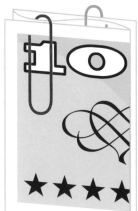

3. Attach one paper clip to the back and middle sections of the 's', and the other to the front and middle sections.

4. Now pull the ends of the note. The clips ping into the air – and join together. You win the money!

★ One of the most famous magic props is a top hat with a false bottom. Magicians pull all kinds of objects – or animals – out of it.

★ In 1918, a magician named Chung Ling Soo died when a specially-made fake gun fired a real bullet, which hit him in the chest.

Whenever you do tricks with everyday objects, borrow them from your audience so they know there are no hidden gimmicks.

Turn the page for more tricks with money.

MONEY MAGIC

Some tricks with coins are tough to learn because they use sleights called **palms**, which involve holding a coin so your hand looks empty. Here are a few tricks that don't take years to perfect!

Money Mind Reader

The secret of this trick is body heat.

1. Before you perform, put about ten coins in a bag, making sure that no two coins are the same. Secretly place the bag in the fridge for a few minutes so the coins are cool – but not cold enough for people to notice.

The coins can be different values, or from different countries, or have varying designs.

2. Ask a friend to pick any coin from the bag, memorize it and keep hold of it. Turn your back as they do this.

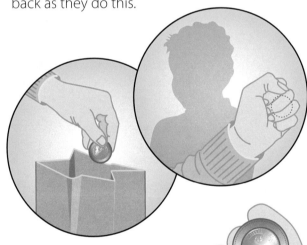

3. Now say you'll work out which coin they picked. Stare hard at their face, as if you're reading their mind.

Do a bit of acting!

4. After a few minutes, pretend you know their coin. Tell them to put it back in the bag, shake it and hand it to you. Quickly feel around in the bag – their coin will be warmer than the rest because they've been holding it.

I think it was… this one!

Find more mind-reading tricks on pages 22 and 23.

Sticky Coin Vanish

For this trick you need a small, lightweight coin, such as a penny.

1. Just before you do this trick, secretly smear a small patch of glue on the back of one hand.

You could do this under the table.

2. Hold the coin in your non-sticky hand and show it to a friend. Let them see that your other hand is empty.

3. Make the sticky hand into a fist and pretend to push the coin inside.

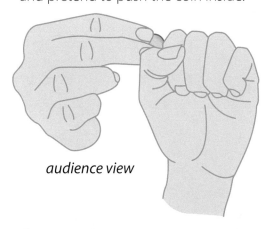

audience view

4. Just push your two fingers into your fist and use your thumb to slide the coin on to the back of your hand. Press it down on the sticky patch.

5. Pull out your fingers, show your hand is empty and wave it over your fist, saying magic words. Open your fist to show that the coin has disappeared.

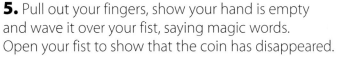

6. To make the coin magically reappear, do the same move in reverse to slide the coin back into your non-sticky hand.

Don't let your friend look at the coin afterwards, or they will notice it's sticky!

SUPER ★ FACTS

★ Some magicians use specially-made extra thin coins when they do palming tricks.

★ Thomas Nelson Downs (1867-1938) called himself the King of Koins. He could hide 60 thin coins in one hand.

PAPER PRANKS

How can you and a friend both stand on the same sheet of A4 paper, but not be able to touch each other? The answer is at the bottom of the page. Now read on for more paper fun.

The Expanding Hole

All you need for this trick is an index card (about 15 x 10 cm) and scissors.

1. Ask a friend if they think you can cut a hole in an index card big enough to fit your whole body through. When they say no, prove them wrong!

2. Fold the card in half. Starting at the crease, cut along the top red line and stop about a centimetre from the end. Do the same at the bottom, cutting along the second to last blue line.

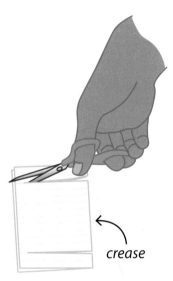

crease

3. Now cut along the crease, between the two outer strips.

4. Starting from the other end of the card, cut along the next blue line at the top and bottom. Stop about a centimetre from the end.

5. Continue cutting along the blue lines in this way, alternating the end you start from. When there are only two lines left, make one last cut along the middle of them.

6. Carefully open out the card. It's now a huge ring – and you can fit through it easily!

Paper Loops

This is a version of a very old, famous trick called the Afghan Bands.

1. Cut two long strips of paper, each about 3 cm wide and 1.5 metres long.

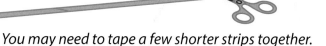

You may need to tape a few shorter strips together.

2. Show a friend the strips, then take one and tape it into a big loop, being careful not to twist it.

3. Make a snip in the middle of the loop with a pair of scissors and cut all the way around, making two thin loops.

4. Bet your friend that they can't copy you. As you talk, pick up the second strip and tape it into a loop – but turn one wrist so you twist the strip.

5. Your friend will cut the strip exactly as you did, but will end up with one huge loop. You were right – they couldn't copy you!

You could do this while asking your friend to pass you a piece of tape.

If you do this trick with a third strip but sneakily twist it twice, your friend will end up with two linked loops!

CARD MAGIC

Every magician needs a few good card tricks. Decks of playing cards are cheap to buy and perfect for quick tricks. Here are some essential card skills.

Cutting cards

One handy skill is knowing how to cut cards. This is a way of seeming to mix up a deck without actually changing the order of the cards.

Practise cutting cards quickly in your hand, so it looks as if you're shuffling them.

1. First, sneak a quick peek at the card on the bottom of the deck. Remember it.

2. Ask a friend to take the top card, memorize it and replace it.

3. Cut the deck. Take some cards off the top of the deck and place them on the table, or in your hand…

4. Cut the cards a few more times, or ask your friend to do it. Then turn them over and look for the card you know. Your friend's card will always be to the right of it.

…then replace the rest of the deck on top.

Royal Couples

Another skill is stacking the deck – in other words, placing cards in a certain order or position. Try this neat trick.

1. Beforehand, take out the kings and queens and arrange them in this order.

2. Slot the kings and queens back in the pack. It doesn't matter exactly where, but the suits MUST stay in the same order.

3. Now say you have a magic method for pairing kings and queens. As you talk, hold the pack face up and casually go through it, putting the kings and queens on two piles as you come to them.

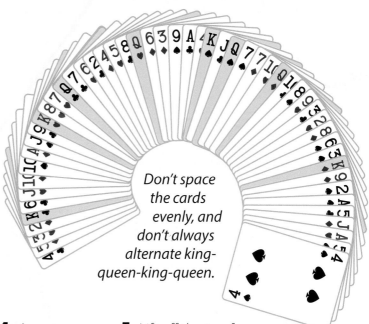

Don't space the cards evenly, and don't always alternate king-queen-king-queen.

People will assume you're picking out cards in a random order.

4. As soon as you've found all eight cards, put one pile on the other, turn them face down and cut them several times.

5. Lift off the top four cards and set them face down, so you have two piles of four. Now click your fingers or say magic words. Turn over the top card from each pile. They're a pair! Do the same with the rest.

SHUFFLING TRICKS

Another vital card skill is knowing how to shuffle. An ordinary, straight shuffle is used to mix a deck of cards, while false shuffles are clever sleights used in all kinds of card tricks.

Straight shuffle

For a straight shuffle, hold the deck in your right hand and rest the cards on your left. Lift most of the deck, then drop a few cards in front of and behind the cards in your left hand. Do it a few times to mix the cards well.

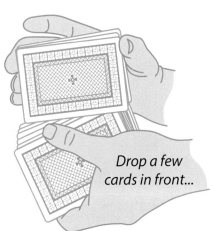

Drop a few cards in front...

...and a few behind.

Hold the deck in your other hand if you're left-handed.

Sneaky stuff

Use a false shuffle to keep cards in place or put them where you want them. You can then make someone pick a certain card. This is called a **force**.

1. Pick up the deck and quickly look at the bottom card.

bottom card

2. Shuffle the cards, making sure you always drop the last few behind the deck in your left hand. The deck seems mixed – but you still know the bottom card.

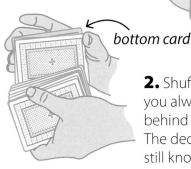

3. To move the bottom card to the top, do a final shuffle, but this time drop the last card, on its own, on top of the deck.

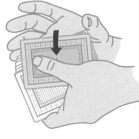

4. Ask a friend to take the top card, memorize it and put it back anywhere in the deck.

5. Give the cards a straight shuffle, fan them out and find the card they chose!

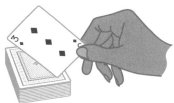

Rising Jacks

Now try using a false shuffle to keep several cards in place.

1. Beforehand, stack the deck so that all four jacks are on top.

2. Do a quick false shuffle by taking a pile of cards from the middle of the pack and dropping them, a few at a time, at the back.

The jacks stay in place.

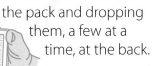

Don't draw attention to false shuffles! Do them quickly and casually, as if you haven't yet started the trick.

3. Cut the pile in half, laying the top half to the right. Cut each pile again, laying the top halves at the ends of the line.

The jacks are on top of this pile.

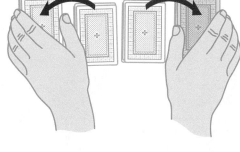

4. Say you'll mix the cards even more. Pick up the first pile and move the top three cards to the bottom, then deal one card on each of the other piles.

5. Put the first pile back in place, then pick up the second pile and do the same – move three cards to the bottom, then deal one card on each of the other piles. Repeat with the third and fourth pile.

6. Say that you can make the jacks rise to the top of any pack. Click your fingers and turn over the four top cards. They're all jacks!

MORE CARD SKILLS

Magicians sometimes hide cards in their clothes before they perform, ready to produce at the right moment. Another trick is to use a specially-made gimmick to make cards disappear. Here's an example of each to try.

The Magic Touch

For this trick, you'll need a shirt with a top pocket and a jacket with an inside pocket. Put the four aces in your shirt pocket beforehand.

1. Ask a friend to shuffle the deck. Show the friend that your jacket pocket is empty, then put the deck inside.

2. Say that your sensitive fingers recognize cards by touch. Reach inside your jacket and pretend to feel in the pocket. Secretly take an ace from your shirt instead.

3. Say that you're trying to find an ace… and pull one out with a flourish! Repeat three times until you've 'found' all the aces.

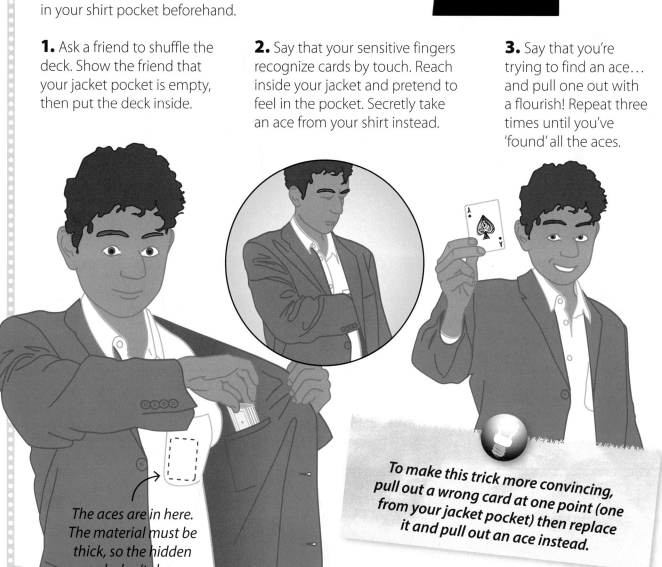

The aces are in here. The material must be thick, so the hidden cards don't show.

To make this trick more convincing, pull out a wrong card at one point (one from your jacket pocket) then replace it and pull out an ace instead.

Card Vanish

Here's a magic box you can make yourself.

1. Find an empty matchbox big enough to hold a playing card. Decorate it.

2. Cut the tray in two, about a third of the way along.

long piece

3. Put the tray back in the sleeve with the long piece at the top.

short piece

4. Ask a friend to choose a card. Open the tray by pushing up the bottom end with your finger, and put the card inside. Hold up the box so your friend can see the card.

5. Push the tray down to close it. Wave your hands or say magic words to make the card vanish. Open the tray again, but push up the bottom end a short way and pull up the top end with your other hand. The card stays in the bottom section of the tray.

Hold the top of the tray as you did in step 5, so it isn't obvious you're opening it differently.

6. Close the tray again and say you'll make the card reappear. This time, push the bottom end of the tray much further, so the card is pushed up too.

ROPE TRICKS

Many classic tricks involve making knots appear or disappear, or cutting a length of rope which then becomes whole again. Rope magic always involves fancy finger work, so practise with these two tricks.

Practise rope tricks looking in a mirror to check the position of your hands, or film yourself. Try to make each move smooth and graceful.

Instant Knot

Impress friends with this move – but don't show it until you can do the second and third steps really quickly.

1. Casually lay a length of rope or string over your hand, like this.

Make this end shorter.

2. Tilt your hand forwards and trap the shorter end between your first and second fingers.

3. Shake your hand hard, once, so the rope falls off – with a knot in it. The more forceful the shake, the tighter the knot and the better the effect.

Magical Mended String

Here's a version of the famous cut and restored rope trick.

tape

1. Beforehand, cut a piece of string about 60 cm long. Cut another about 10 cm long and tape it into a loop.

2. With the loop hidden in one hand, show a friend the long piece of string.

Hold both hands in the same way, so it isn't obvious you're hiding something.

3. Use the thumb and first finger of your free hand to take the long string in the middle and pass it to the other hand. As you grasp it, push up the hidden loop, so it seems to be part of the long string.

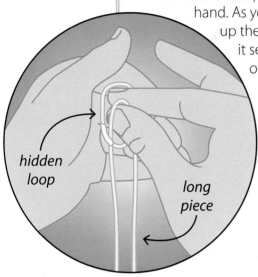

hidden loop

long piece

4. Hold the string tightly in your fist and ask your friend to cut the loop.

5. Poke the cut ends into your fist, say magic words and then slowly and dramatically pull out the long string to show it's whole again. Keep the short piece hidden in your lower hand.

short piece hidden here

Do this trick at a table so you can drop the string out of sight on to your lap.

MIND-READING MAGIC

Mind-reading tricks are a type of magic called mentalism, in which a magician (called a mentalist) claims to have incredible mind power. They are fun because you can do lots of acting as you pretend to read your friends' deepest thoughts!

Word Genius

This trick relies on a clever bit of maths that leads your friend to the number nine. Give them a calculator if you think they might get the sum wrong!

1. Beforehand, choose a book or magazine and memorize the first word on page nine.

2. Ask a friend to write down any four digits. Now ask them to rearrange the digits and write them again, then subtract the second set from the first.

television

9

$$7352$$
$$-5237$$
$$\overline{2115}$$

Make sure you don't see any of this.

3. Ask them to add the four new digits together. If this gives them a two-digit number, tell them to add the two. They need to finish with a one-digit number.

$$2+1+1+5=9$$

4. Casually pick up the book or magazine. Tell your friend to turn to the page matching their number and memorize the first word.

5. Stare at your friend and concentrate hard. Then announce or write the word you memorized.

For extra effect, pretend to 'see' the word gradually.

It's hazy… wait, I can see a screen… a computer? No! A television!

To make this even more impressive, memorize words from several books, then let your friend pick whichever one they want.

Double acts

Imagine this: at a party, you put a coin on the table and say that someone must take it while you're out of the room. When you return, you know who has the coin. How? Because one of your friends is your secret assistant!

The key is to agree a code beforehand. Your friend might rub their nose to indicate one friend, or cross their legs to mean another, and so on. Or they could use code words that begin with the same letter as people's names, as in, "This should be interesting," for Isobel.

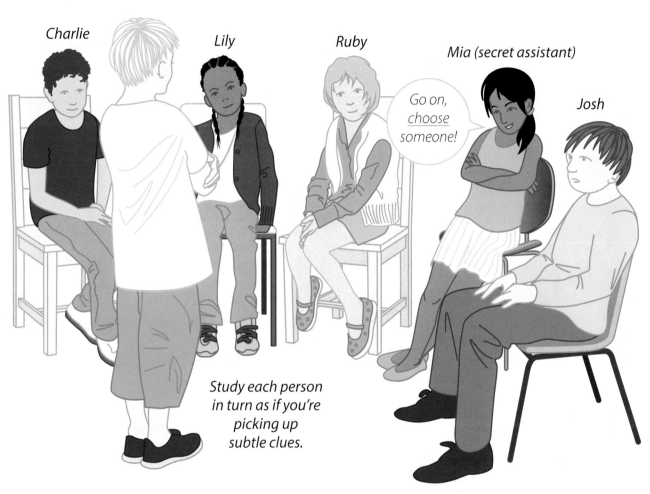

Charlie   Lily   Ruby   Mia (secret assistant)   Josh

Go on, choose someone!

Study each person in turn as if you're picking up subtle clues.

Who has the coin? The answer is at the bottom.

SUPER ★ FACTS

★ Telepathy is a double act in which two people use a code to pretend to read each other's minds.

★ Hypnotism is a form of mentalism in which people can be persuaded by a magician to alter their behaviour or thoughts.

★ A famous mentalism trick is bending metal using mind power. It usually involves clever sleights and brilliant misdirection.

Charlie has the coin. The code word was 'choose'.

SCIENCE MAGIC

Some tricks work every time because they're not really tricks at all – they rely on quirky laws of science. Entertain your friends with these amazing experiments, and learn some fascinating scientific facts, too.

Upward Water

Tell a friend you can make water flow up into a glass.

1. Fix a match upright in the middle of a saucer using a blob of modelling clay. Fill the saucer with water. Add a drop of food colouring if you want the water to show up better.

Be extremely careful when using matches. Get adult help if you need it.

2. Light the match with another match, then immediately put a small glass on top.

3. Water flows up into the glass, and stays there even when the match has gone out!

This works because the match uses the **oxygen** in the glass to burn. This creates a **vacuum**, which sucks in water through the space between the glass and the saucer.

Soap Power

Prove to a friend that soap can be used as fuel.

1. Cut a small piece of card into a simple boat shape. Float it in a large bowl of water. Tell a friend you can turn it into a speedboat.

2. Take the boat out of the water and put a blob of liquid soap on the back part.

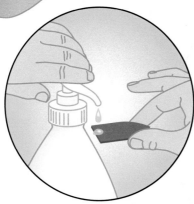

3. Place it at the edge of the bowl and it will speed across the water.

If you want to do this again, you'll need fresh water.

This works because of surface tension. The water forms a very thin skin on which things float. The soap breaks the skin and it pulls away to the sides of the bowl, taking the boat with it.

Floating Arm

Tell a friend your magical powers are so strong that you can control their body!

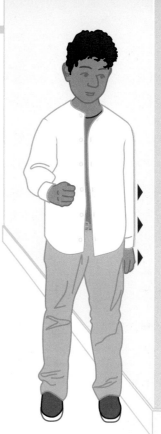

1. Ask your friend to stand with one arm pressed against a wall, pushing with their arm (not their whole body) as if they're trying to move the wall. Count to 20.

2. Now ask them to step away and let their arms hang relaxed at their sides. Point at the arm that was pressed against the wall and order it to rise. Sure enough, the arm will magically lift.

This trick works because your friend's arm muscles become so used to pushing against the wall, they continue to push even when the wall isn't there. It's a strange feeling – try it yourself and see!

EXTREME MAGIC

Some professional magicians grab their audience's attention by performing daring, gruesome or over-the-top stunts. Other magicians believe that simpler, low-key sleights are far more effective. What do you think?

Going to pieces

The famous trick in which a magician saws an assistant in half inside a box caused a sensation when it was first performed in 1921. Since then, magicians have invented many new versions, for example using spinning circular saws, or severing two people then reassembling them so that each has the other's legs!

▲ *Tricks like these use real knives – but you can be sure the box isn't an ordinary one!*

This isn't the kind of trick to try out at home.

Ouch!

Some magicians love to shock audiences by pretending to injure themselves. These horribly realistic tricks are usually done with the help of special props and a glue called rubber cement, which sticks to itself but nothing else.

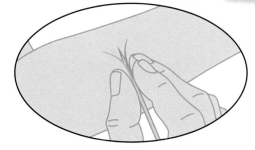
Rubber cement contains hazardous substances and is highly flammable. It's not for beginners!

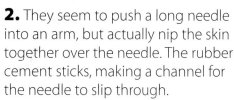

1. First, the magician secretly brushes rubber cement on their skin. It dries clear and smooth, so it can't be seen.

2. They seem to push a long needle into an arm, but actually nip the skin together over the needle. The rubber cement sticks, making a channel for the needle to slip through.

3. The needle is hollow, with fake blood in one end. The magician squeezes the end and blood oozes out of a tiny hole in the needle.

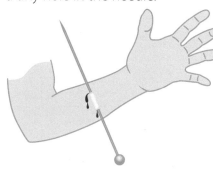

Great escapes

Some magicians perform risky **escapology** routines, freeing themselves from ropes, handcuffs, cages, sacks and boxes – or all of these at once. They use a combination of gimmicks, sleight of hand (for example tying false knots) and skills such as picking locks and squeezing through tight spaces.

Endurance feats

A few magicians take escapology ideas further and perform acts of extreme endurance – for example, being buried alive, encased in ice or submerged in a water tank. It's hard to tell whether illusions are involved or whether these are genuine – and very dangerous – stunts.

► *The most famous escapologist was a Hungarian magician called Harry Houdini.*

▲ *David Blaine has performed many endurance feats, including spending seven days in a water-filled ball.*

WHAT NEXT?

The secret to becoming a great magician is simple: practise! Carry cards and other small props in your pocket and get them out whenever you have a spare minute. Look for good tricks in books and online, and pick ones that look fun to try.

Planning an act

Once you know lots of tricks, try staging a proper magic act for your friends and family, at home or at school. Choose a variety of tricks, and think about where your audience will sit – it's no good doing coin or card magic if people aren't close enough to see!

Dressing up

How you look is important, as it can make people pay attention, and give you more confidence, too. Pick a costume that fits the style of your act – for example, if you're doing card tricks, try a smart suit and gloves. For a mind-reading show, sweeping robes and a wig can make you look more mysterious.

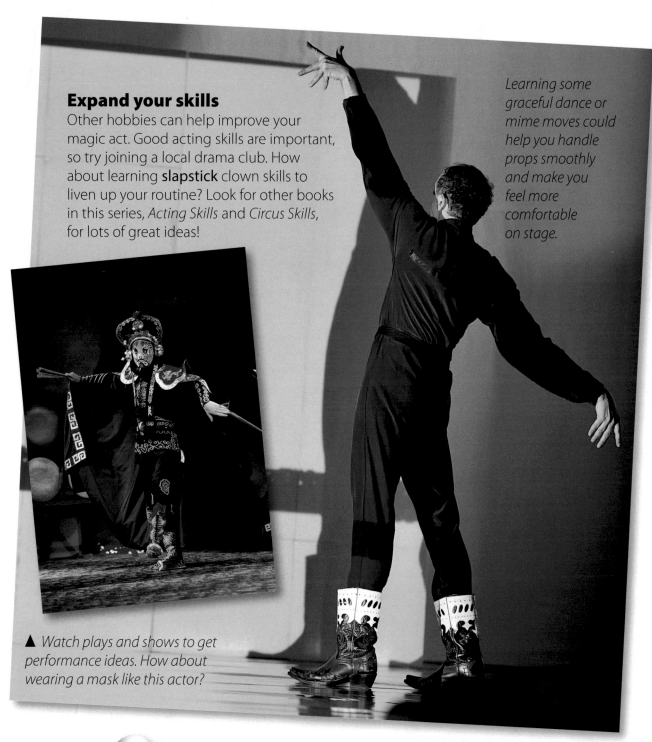

Expand your skills

Other hobbies can help improve your magic act. Good acting skills are important, so try joining a local drama club. How about learning **slapstick** clown skills to liven up your routine? Look for other books in this series, *Acting Skills* and *Circus Skills*, for lots of great ideas!

Learning some graceful dance or mime moves could help you handle props smoothly and make you feel more comfortable on stage.

▲ *Watch plays and shows to get performance ideas. How about wearing a mask like this actor?*

Watch other magicians to get ideas for your own performance. But don't just copy them – find your own style.

A magic career

Magic isn't something you can study at school, so if you're serious about a career as a magician, keep practising in your spare time. Offer to perform at parties or in children's hospitals. Look for talent competitions to enter. If you're really skilled, you may get booked for more work. Good luck!

GLOSSARY

conjuror
Another word for magician. Traditionally, conjurors perform tricks such as making things appear or disappear.

escapology
A skill that involves escaping from constraints or unsafe places. Escapologists often put themselves in real danger, so this isn't a type of magic you should try yourself.

force
A way of seeming to offer someone a free choice when in fact you make sure they pick one particular thing. Forces are used a lot in magic tricks.

gimmick
A magic prop with a secret part or mechanism – for example, a false bottom or hidden spring – that makes a trick work.

illusion
An effect that tricks you into thinking something impossible is happening.

joker
A card that usually has a picture of a jester on it. Jokers can be used to replace lost or damaged cards. Unless your trick needs them, take the jokers out of the deck before you begin.

levitating
Suspending a person or object in the air without any visible support, so they seem to defy gravity.

mentalism
Magic tricks that appear to rely on a magician's amazing mental powers.

oxygen
An invisible gas in the air around us. We breathe oxygen, and fire uses oxygen to burn.

palm
A way of hiding an object, such as a coin or a card, in the palm of your hand. A back palm involves hiding something on the back of your hand, gripping the edges between your fingers.

patter
Prepared, practised speech that magicians use when performing tricks. Always work out your patter before you perform.

slapstick
Silly, funny and over-the-top. Some magicians pretend to be clumsy clowns to keep their audience entertained and also to distract them from sneaky sleights.

vacuum
An enclosed space from which gas has been removed.

USEFUL WEBSITES

www.activitytv.com/magic-tricks-for-kids
Find helpful video tutorials and clear instructions for
all kinds of tricks. Search by skill level or browse them all.

www.theyoungmagiciansclub.co.uk
Learn about the Young Magician's Club, a group for 10- to 18-year-olds, run by a famous
magic society called the Magic Circle. There is a fee to join, but members then receive
newsletters, magazines, free tricks and advice from a panel of magic experts.

www.magictricks.com/library
Learn who's who in the world of magic! Read about famous magicians of the past
and the amazing tricks they invented.

www.card-trick.com/free_card_tricks.htm
Discover lots of new card tricks. Choose self-working tricks or more difficult sleight of hand moves.

www.escapology.co.uk
Read more about escapology and famous escapologists,
then watch videos of impressive escapes.

www.layhands.com/ScienceTricks/Index.htm
Search pages of fun, fascinating and easy-to-do science
tricks, games and puzzles.

INDEX

For Katie, Sophie and Sam – M.W.
For Team 'de Grey' – S.V.

This paperback edition first published in 2010 by Andersen Press Ltd.
First published in Great Britain in 2008 by Andersen Press Ltd., 20 Vauxhall Bridge Road, London SW1V 2SA.
Published in Australia by Random House Australia Pty., Level 3, 100 Pacific Highway, North Sydney, NSW 2060.
Text copyright © Martin Waddell, 2008. Illustration copyright © Susan Varley, 2008.
The rights of Martin Waddell and Susan Varley to be identified as the author and illustrator of this
work have been asserted by them in accordance with the Copyright, Designs and Patents Act, 1988.
All rights reserved. Colour separated in Switzerland by Photolitho AG, Zürich.
Printed and bound in Singapore by Tien Wah Press.

10   9   8   7   6   5   4   3   2   1

British Library Cataloguing in Publication Data available.

ISBN 978 1 84270 819 4
This book has been printed on acid-free paper

CAPTAIN SMALL PIG

Martin Waddell   Susan Varley

ANDERSEN PRESS

One day Old Goat and Turkey took Small Pig down to Blue Lake.
They found a little red boat.
"I want to go for a row!" Small Pig said, dancing about.
"Turkeys don't go in boats," Turkey said.
"Neither do goats," said Old Goat, but he climbed into the boat,
and they rowed off on Blue Lake.

"I want to fish for whales!" said Small Pig.

"There aren't any whales in Blue Lake," said Turkey.

"There might be a very small whale," said Old Goat, and he tied a string to an oar, so Small Pig could try his whale fishing.

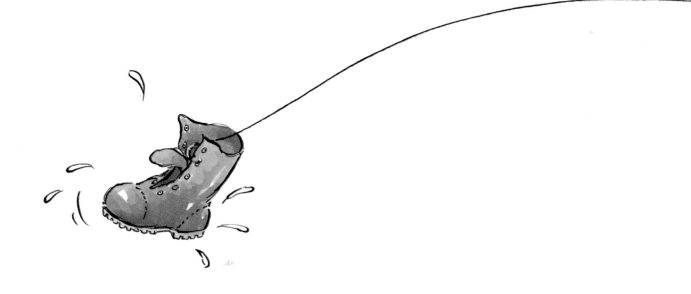

Small Pig didn't catch any whales,
but he caught an old boot,
which was almost as good . . .
you can store lots of things in a boot.

"I want to row now!" said Small Pig.

"You're too small to row!" Turkey objected.

"Of course you can row!" said Old Goat.

Small Pig could only manage one oar at time so he rowed . . .

round and round . . .

. . . round and round . . . round and round . . .

but he rowed the boat all by himself.

"I'm Captain Commander!" Small Pig said.
Turkey just nodded his head, sleepily.
"Aye aye, Captain Small Pig!" said Old Goat.
"You are in charge of this boat!"

"But I'm too tired to row any more!" Small Pig said.

"I knew you would be!" said Turkey.

"Just let the boat drift," yawned Old Goat sleepily.

"But keep your hand on the tiller!"

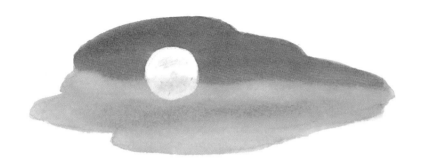

As the moon rose, the boat drifted back through the reeds, toward the shore.

Small Pig was . . . sort of . . . steering the boat. And then . . . Small Pig . . . sort of . . . wasn't steering the boat. He'd fallen asleep holding his boot.

The boat was . . . sort of . . . steering itself.

"My turn to steer!" sighed old Goat. He shifted the sleeping Small Pig, and took over the tiller.

As they drew towards the jetty the boat rocked . . .

one way . . . .

and then the other . . . until . . .

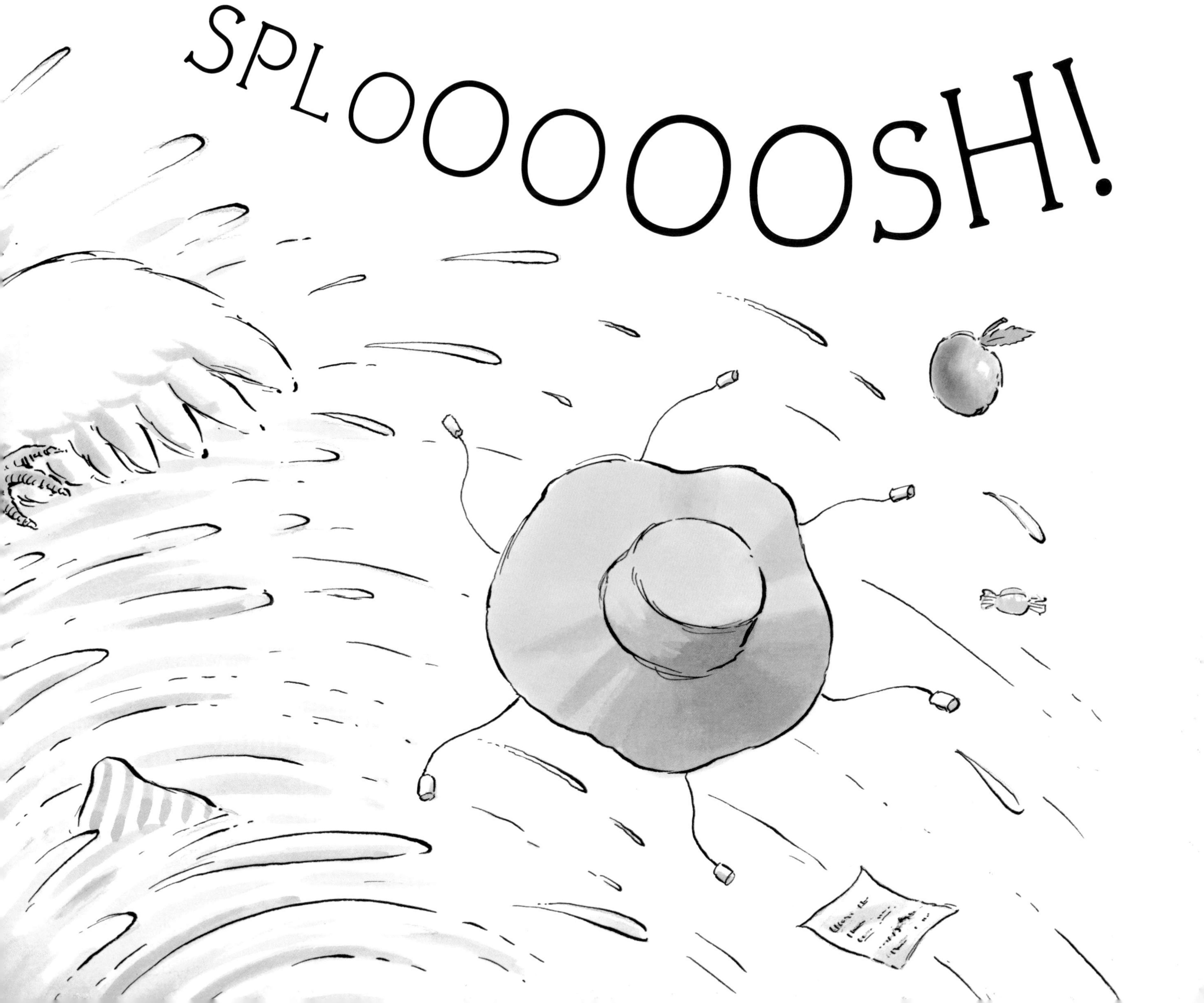
SPLOOOOOSH!

"GRRR . . .

OH-AH . . .

GLUG-UG!" spluttered Turkey.

"*Shhhhh!* We mustn't wake up Captain Small Pig!" Old Goat
warned Turkey.

They carried Small Pig all the way home, wrapped warm in a rug,
and they tucked him up cosy in bed.

Small Pig slept . . . and he dreamt . . . of a lovely day out
in a boat with good friends on Blue Lake . . .

. . . the day he was Captain Small Pig.

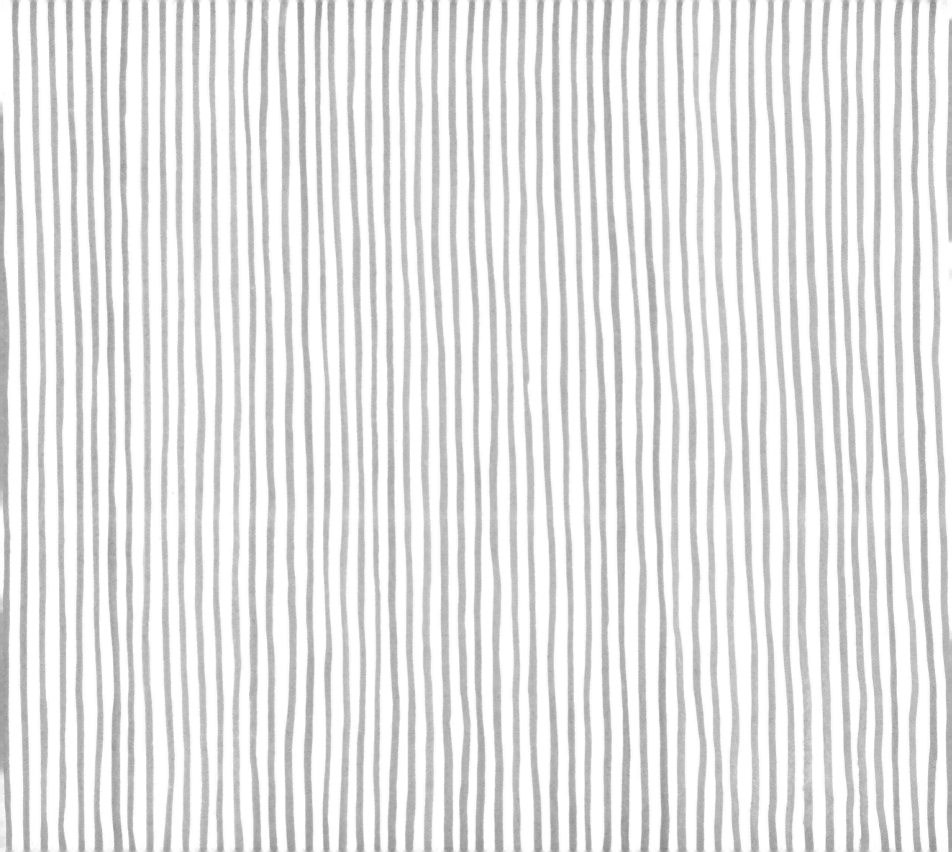

Other books by Susan Varley:

BADGER'S PARTING GIFTS

THE MONSTER BED (text by Jeanne Willis)